"Natasha's heart beats in rhythm with that of her Creator. When she ministers with her music, the hearts of her audience connect with the great God we serve. I commend her for writing a devotional journal to invite readers into a greater love and worship of our Lord Jesus!"
-- Anita Carmen, Founder and President of Inspire Women
and author of *A Daughter's Destiny*

"This engaging devotional journal will enable you to better understand how to experience God's presence."
--Barry C. Black, Chaplain of the U.S. Senate

"A beautiful book and beautiful songs all from the special heart of a very special lady. Get ready to be blessed."
--Dr. John Bisagno, Pastor Emeritus,
Houston's First Baptist Church

"Natasha is a powerfully anointed woman of God whose music and teachings usher the Presence of God into people's lives. Her Whisper Your Secrets *music CD and devotional journal will bless you tremendously and give you fresh wind, fresh fire, and fresh revelation."*
--Steve Austin, Senior Director & Pastor at Lakewood Church

"Natasha takes readers on an intimate journey into the truth about who God is and who He's created us to be. Whether you are longing to discover God or develop a deeper relationship with God, read this book and listen to the accompanying music to start your journey today."
--Mike Reiszner, Founder of Coreluv International

"Natasha's book created a unique experience for me as the reader. She covers a broad range of practical theology yet brings each chapter to life by designing brilliant incisive questions and opportunities to journal. It is both easy to work with and yet profound. I encourage you to read this and begin exploring your spiritual life as you fill out your own personal reflections."
-- Dr. Lance Wallnau, Lance Learning Group

*"Attorney, Worshiper, Passionate pursuer of the Lord--
these describe not only Natasha's skills but also her essence.
As an attorney, Natasha skillfully presents her case in a very inspiring,
simple and insightful manner, and as a living Worshiper, Natasha's deep
passionate pursuit to know the Lord is reflected in her lyrics and style of
worship music. She has uniquely brought all these gifts together in a very
clear and anointed way through* Whisper Your Secrets *book and accompanying music. I know these tools will not only engage the reader and
listener into deeper reflective thought, but also into a heartfelt desire to
know the Lord in a richer and more meaningful way.*

*My wife, Lisa, spent many years in the music entertainment industry
as a programmer in a major U.S. market and one who owned her own
record label. She is not one to give kudos easily when asked to give input
to music she is requested to listen to. She shared with me that she enjoyed
Natasha's music that accompanies her book, and she sensed the Lord's
inspiration and hand on it in a unique way. She listened to the accompanying music in various settings and felt it was a perfect match which
ushered in peace as she spent time with the journal."*

--Dr. Doug Stringer, Founder/President Somebody Cares America,
Somebody Cares International and Turning Point Ministries International
Houston, Texas

Whisper
Your
Secrets

A Devotional Journal

natasha

Whisper Your Secrets: A Devotional Journal

By *natasha*

As One Light Publishing
945 McKinney St. #423
Houston, Texas 77002

Unless otherwise noted, all scripture quotations are taken from The NET Bible ®. For more information, visit www.bible.org.

Library of Congress Control Number: 2017902598
ISBN: 978-0-692-85106-7
Printed in the United States of America.

ABOUT THE AUTHOR

An unquenchable fire blazes within Natasha for people to know and experience God. Her desire is for believers to become one with God in order to reflect Him and, thus, *Live As One Light*. Natasha graduated with a Masters of Divinity from Southwestern Baptist Theological Seminary and currently teaches at her home church. While in seminary, she started Soulcheck, a multi-cultural multi-denominational gathering that brought the Body of Christ together in Houston, Seattle, and Guam to worship the Lord for 12 hours in different languages and styles. She also leads worship and intercession at different churches and ministries and loves writing songs and singing. She has a passion for prayer, equipping believers in the marketplace, and unifying the Body of Christ. She is an attorney by trade and in the summer of 2014 married her loving and supportive husband Timothy. In 2016, they welcomed their precious daughter. She zealously loves God and constantly pours out her talents and skills for the spreading of the gospel and to aid other ministries. The Lord has blessed her to work with the multi-cultural, multi-generational, multi-denominational body of Christ.

DEDICATION

Dedicated to all the precious people that I have encountered on my faith journey. Thank you for who you are. Whether we smiled, spoke, partnered, encouraged, worked, or served together, you are treasured and unforgettable.

ACKNOWLEDGEMENTS

I acknowledge my precious daughter and my loving husband who have been the catalysts for this project.

TABLE *of* CONTENTS

PREFACE 13

INSTRUCTIONS TO ACCESS MUSIC..14

PART 1: IMPORTANT QUESTIONS

Session 1: Who are You? 17

Session 2: What is Your Raw Response? 23

Session 3: What is God Longing For? 27

Session 4: What To Do Now? 31

Session 5: What is Your Attitude? 35

PART 2:   TIME FOR BREAKTHROUGH

Session 6:   Expose Lies, Receive Truth 39

Session 7:   Repent 43

Session 8:   Forgive..49

Session 9:   Break Agreement 53

Session 10: Act in an Opposite Spirit 59

Session 11: No Discussion, Just Rebuke 63

Session 12: Be Unoffendable 67

Session 13: Pray the Word...71

PART 3:   WALKING IN THE SPIRIT

Session 14: The Power of Love...77

Session 15: The Power of Worship 85

Session 16: The Power of Speaking Life 89

Session 17: The Blessing of Sacrifice.....................................95

Session 18: The Blessing of Obedience 99

Session 19: The Blessing of Faith...103

PART 4:   RELY ON THIS

Session 20: Rest Assured of God..109

Session 21: Listen to the Holy Spirit.....................................113

APPENDIX: LYRICS

Freedom 121
Whisper Your Secrets 123
Child of God 125
No Turning Back 127
Anything for You 129

PREFACE

Who really cares? God does. He has reached through time and space and entered into our reality on countless occasions. Whether talking through a burning bush, an angel, or a donkey, God has things to say because He cares. The question is: Do we care enough to listen?

Communication is key to a vibrant relationship. *Whisper Your Secrets: A Devotional Journal* cultivates an exchange of whispers between God and us. As we spill the secret things of our heart, God will respond by sharing His heart. Especially with the unveiling of confusion, anger, violence, lust, depression, injustice, and wickedness in our society and our hearts, we need to decipher God's voice and live from a place of knowing how His Kingdom operates.

By crafting an interactive experience of reading, responding, praying, and listening, the book challenges the reader to introspectively look at our souls, communicate with the Lord, and take action. Concurrently, the music creates a peaceful environment while providing positive reinforcement of the truths shared. The book allows the reader in Part 1 to substantiate their identity in God, in Part 2 to wrestle with their soul and be victorious, in Part 3 to align themselves with the Spirit, and in Part 4 to launch into a new season of intimacy, faith, and trust in the Lord.

God cares. We care. Let's start this 21 Session adventure and begin the interchange of whispering secrets. This self-paced experience will be a point of reference for the rest of our lives.

Blessings!

natasha

INSTRUCTIONS
TO ACCESS MUSIC

Please, listen to and/or download (for free) the accompanying original music by going to www.NatashaMinistries.com/wys.

Part 1:

IMPORTANT QUESTIONS

WHO ARE YOU?

Describe yourself in three words.

_____

_____

_____

Describe yourself five years ago in three words.

_____

_____

_____

Describe yourself ten years ago in three words.

_____

_____

_____

In three words, describe yourself when _____

_____ (a pivotal event) happened.

_____

_____

_____

Describe yourself during _____in three words.

_____

_____

_____

Each word you wrote embodies a label either self-imposed or accepted from others. The various labels over time show the evolution of how you self-identify. The label-forming process influenced by painful ordeals, edifying experiences, family, people in authority, friends, strangers, environments, choices, behaviors, or beliefs reflects how you view yourself. Review your labels. By what standard should you use to evaluate what you have written down? What has been your true identity throughout all those years?

Well, there is a three-word label that does not change and is true for you throughout your life:

Loved. Valued. Desired.

God, the Creator and Ruler of the Universe, loves, values, and desires you. This is not cliché; this is truth. He knew you before you were in your mother's womb and wants to commune with you daily (Jer. 1:5, 1 Thess. 5:16-18). He also happens to be the most famous living being ever. More books have been written about Him, more songs have been sung regarding Him, and more gatherings have been organized for Him than any other human. He is the most powerful person in the world; He created it. Whomever calls upon His name shall be saved (Acts 2:21). He is Perfect, Holy, and Righteous; someone whom you can trust 100%. He always fulfills His word—perfectly Faithful and Just. Therefore, the fact that He labels you as "Loved. Valued. Desired." means something. That truth can refresh you in a tired moment, invigorate you in a saddened state, heal wounds, remove the stain of regret, spur you towards holiness and obedience, or just put a simile on your face.

How do you know that this is true? Well, let me explain what God did for you:

For God so LOVED the world (YOU) that He gave His only begotten Son (Jesus), that whoever believes in Him should not perish but have everlasting life (John 3:16). God LOVED YOU so much that He allowed His own Son to take the puishment for your sins—Jesus bore our sins, my sins, your sins—as His own (1 Pet. 2:22-24). That is why Jesus was beaten, whipped, crucified, and sent to hell. Someone had to suffer God's just and holy wrath for those sins, and God VALUED YOU so much that He allowed His Son to take your punishment. Simultaneously, Jesus, God's Son, DESIRED you so much that He chose to endure physical, emotional, and mental torture in order to be with you for eternity. His LOVE, VALUE, and DESIRE for you is not mere words, but sealed with action.

This beautiful story, though, does not end in suffering, but in great joy because after suffering on the cross and being in hell for three days, Jesus was resurrected. That is why He is called the Living God. He is alive. He overcame death and the grave because He Himself was sinless, and now sits at the right hand of the Father whom has given Him all power and authority in heaven and in earth (Mark 16:19). By Jesus accepting God's will for Him to endure your punishment for your sins, you are able to have an eternal relationship with God, the Creator of Life, that starts while you are alive on the earth. How awesome is that! Joy has no limits when you fully understand who you have relationship with and how He views you. Allow that truth to permeate you: God loves, values, and desires you!

Conversation Starters with God:

"Lord, I desire to know the fullness of the Love you have for me. In faith, I believe You will open my understanding to every aspect of Your Love, Value and Desire for me. I look forward to experiencing the full freedom of knowing the truth of who I am to and in You."

Meditate on These Scriptures
while Listening to "Freedom":

But God shows His love for us in that while we were still sinners, Christ died for us (Rom. 5:8).

For He chose us in Christ before the foundation of the world that we may be holy and unblemished in His sight in love. He did this by predestining us to adoption as His sons through Jesus Christ,

according to the pleasure of His will—to the praise of the glory of His grace that He has freely bestowed on us in His dearly loved Son. In Him we have redemption [He purchased our freedom.] through His blood, the forgiveness of our trespasses, according to the riches of His grace that He lavished on us in all wisdom and insight (Eph. 1:4-8).

In all these things we have complete victory through Him who loved us. For I am sure that neither death nor life, nor angels nor heavenly rulers, nor things that are present, nor things to come, nor powers, nor height, nor depth, nor anything else in creation will be able to separate us from the love of God in Christ Jesus our Lord (Rom. 8:37-39).

But God, being rich in mercy, because of His great love with which He loved us, even though we were dead in transgressions, made us alive together with Christ—by grace you are saved!—and He raised us up with Him and seated us with Him in the heavenly realms in Christ Jesus, to demonstrate in the coming ages the surpassing wealth of His grace in kindness toward us in Christ Jesus. For by grace you are saved through faith, and this is not from yourselves, it is the gift of God; it is not from works, so that no one can boast. For we are His workmanship, having been created in Christ Jesus for good works that God prepared beforehand so we may do them (Eph. 2:4-10).

Therefore I tell you, do not worry about your life, what you will eat or drink, or about your body, what you will wear. Isn't there more to life than food and more to the body than clothing? Look at the birds in the sky: They do not sow, or reap, or gather into barns, yet your heavenly Father feeds them. Aren't you more valuable than they are? And which of you by worrying can add even one hour to

his life? Why do you worry about clothing? Think about how the flowers of the field grow; they do not work or spin. Yet I tell you that not even Solomon in all his glory was clothed like one of these! And if this is how God clothes the wild grass, which is here today and tomorrow is tossed into the fire to heat the oven, won't He clothe you even more, you people of little faith? So then, don't worry saying, "What will we eat?" or "What will we drink?" or "What will we wear?" For the unconverted pursue these things, and your heavenly Father knows that you need them. But above all pursue His kingdom and righteousness, and all these things will be given to you as well. So then, do not worry about tomorrow, for tomorrow will worry about itself. Today has enough trouble of its own (Matt. 6:25-34).

When the kindness of God our Savior and His love for mankind appeared, He saved us not by works of righteousness that we have done but on the basis of His mercy, through the washing of the new birth and the renewing of the Holy Spirit, whom He poured out on us in full measure through Jesus Christ our Savior. And so, since we have been justified by His grace, we become heirs with the confident expectation of eternal life (Titus 3:4-7).

You are altogether beautiful, my darling! There is no blemish in you! (Song of Sol. 4:7).

Session 2:

WHAT IS YOUR RAW RESPONSE?

In Session 1, you learned about God's actions that backed His three-word label for you: "Loved. Valued. Desired." The question is: "What is your response to Him?"

_____

_____

_____

_____

_____

May I tell you how He wants you to respond? He wants you to love, value, and desire Him back. Can you imagine the most powerful God in the universe wants you to love, value, and desire Him? Well, for some, that statement dredges up resentment, bitterness, old hurts, wounds, hatred, anger, and even violence. Why don't you take some time and write out every feeling, and thought, whether it be animosity or tenderness towards the Lord. Use another sheet of paper if necessary. What do you feel when you hear that the Lord wants you to love Him?

_____

_____

_____

_____

_____

_____

_____

_____

_____

_____

Everything you wrote, the Lord wanted to hear. He values what you think and feel because He loves you. He desires peace to reign in the relationship between you and Him. He wants you to know that you can trust Him and He will be faithful to you. Some things that happen in life are hard to understand, and He knows that. Your anger, shame, hurt, etc., toward Him does not change His heart toward you. He loves you with an everlasting love.

Will you do something? Will you give those hurtful situations to Him? Will you be brave and dive deep within your soul and talk with Him about your circumstances? Will you give them to Him?

_____

_____

_____

_____

_____

_____

_____

_____

_____

_____

_____

_____

Conversation Starters with God:

"Lord, I said it. Oh, I said it—all the good, the bad, and the ugly. There it is. I am sure I will have more to share with You later. In faith, I'm giving everything to You now. I don't want to hold on to it anymore. I don't want to struggle loving You. I want to be free! Lord, please, help me to love, value, and desire You like You want me to. Speak to me; I am listening. I know You say in Jeremiah 33:3 that You will tell me great and unsearchable things I do not know when I call on You. Lord, I'm calling on You right now."

Meditate on These Scriptures
& Listen to "Whisper Your Secrets":

Jesus said to him, "Love the Lord your God with all your heart, with all your soul, and with all your mind" (Matt. 22:37).

Now, Israel, what does the Lord your God require of you except to revere him, to obey all his commandments, to love him, to serve him with all your mind and being (Deut. 10:12).

Do not love the world or the things in the world. If anyone loves the world, the love of the Father is not in him, because all that is in the world (the desire of the flesh and the desire of the eyes and the arrogance produced by material possessions) is not from the Father, but is from the world. And the world is passing away with all its desires, but the person who does the will of God remains forever (1 John 2:15-17).

See what sort of love the Father has given to us: that we should be called God's children—and indeed we are! For this reason the world

does not know us: because it did not know Him (1 John 3:1).

For people will be lovers of themselves, lovers of money, boastful, arrogant, blasphemers, disobedient to parents, ungrateful, unholy, unloving, irreconcilable, slanderers, without self-control, savage, opposed to what is good, treacherous, reckless, conceited, loving pleasure rather than loving God. They will maintain the outward appearance of religion but will have repudiated its power. So avoid people like these (2 Tim. 3:2-5).

For we must all appear before the judgment seat of Christ, so that each one may be paid back according to what he has done while in the body, whether good or evil (2 Cor. 5:10).

The person who does not love does not know God, because God is love (1 John 4:8).

For the Lord God is our sovereign protector. The Lord bestows favor and honor; He withholds no good thing from those who have integrity (Ps. 84:11).

The Lord is near the brokenhearted; He delivers those who are discouraged (Ps. 34:18).

WHAT IS GOD LONGING FOR?

In Session 2 you were able to pour out your response to the Lord labeling you as "Loved. Valued. Desired." Yes, God would like reciprocally to be loved, valued, and desired; but what is God longing for? Why does He have these personal emotions towards you? God longs for you to be intimate with Him. He wants to walk in the cool of the garden with you like He did with Adam. Adam's sin caused a separation between him and God. After eating from the Tree of Knowledge of Good and Evil, Adam no longer walked in the garden with the Lord. He was thrown out of the garden (Gen. 2:4-3:24). Sin ended the intimacy. That is why Jesus Christ ultimately died for our sins—so intimacy could be regained. By Jesus Christ enduring the just wrath of God for the sins of the world, intimacy was restored between the world and God.

So, how do we plug into this new intimacy? What do you think? How do we become intimate with God?

_____

_____

_____

_____

_____

If you responded with, "By accepting Jesus Christ as Lord and Savior," you got the answer right! When you accept Jesus as Savior, you are saying, "Yes, Jesus Christ saved me from experiencing God's just wrath for my sins (Rom. 5:9). Jesus took your punishment and because of that you will not endure the eternal punishment of hell. When you accept Jesus as Lord, it means that you decide to become His disciple. As a disciple, you desire to follow His commandments and His ways; you long for intimacy because you desire to know the heart and voice of God. As a disciple, your very nature begins to change because God, as the Holy Spirit, now dwells in you, and you begin to desire what the Lord desires (1 Cor. 3:16; 2 Cor. 5:17; Rom. 8). Have you had that moment when you accepted Jesus Christ? If you have, describe it:

_____

_____

_____

_____

_____

If you have not, pray the following declaration and tell a pastor and/or a believer about your prayer:

"Jesus, I believe that you died for my sins. I accept you as my Savior. I also accept you as my Lord. I desire to be Your disciple. Teach me; lead me; groom me. I desire to serve You and be intimate with You for the rest of my life."

The angels are rejoicing with you! You are now a Child of God. When you accept Jesus, you receive God as your Heavenly Father and Holy Spirit as your Guide and Counselor. It is a three-in-one package: three persons— one God. God by His Spirit (the Holy Spirit) impregnated a woman (put Himself in the egg) who then gave birth to Jesus, who was 100% man and 100% divine. When you accept Jesus as your Savior and Lord, God then resides in you in the form of the Holy Spirit. God the Father, Jesus the Son, and Holy Spirit work in absolute unity (as one) so that their divine will comes to pass.

Conversation Starters with God:

"Since I'm your Child, Lord, rear me! I avail myself to your molding, encouragement, and discipline. Place a hunger in me for Your Word and reveal Yourself to me. I love You."

OR

"God, I'm not there yet, but I still want to know about you. Please, continue to speak to me and draw me closer to You. Reveal Yourself to me in such a way that all barriers are broken and that I can wholeheartedly embrace you and become a Child of God."

Meditate on These Scriptures
& Listen to "Child of God":

**Note: Being a Son of God is synonymous with being a Child of God. "Son" has no reference to gender, it relates to both males and females like "Bride of Christ" relates to both males and females.

But to all who have received Him—those who believe in His name—He has given the right to become God's children (John 1:12).

For in Christ Jesus you are all sons of God through faith (Gal. 3:26).

And if children, then heirs (namely, heirs of God and also fellow heirs with Christ)—if indeed we suffer with Him so we may also be glorified with Him (Rom. 8:17).

So you are no longer a slave but a son, and if you are a son, then you are also an heir through God (Gal. 4:7).

Blessed are the peacemakers, for they will be called the children of God (Matt. 5:9).

Do everything without grumbling or arguing, so that you may be blameless and pure, children of God without blemish though you live in a crooked and perverse society, in which you shine as lights in the world by holding on to the word of life so that on the day of Christ I will have a reason to boast that I did not run in vain nor labor in vain (Phil. 2:14-16).

Session 4:

WHAT TO DO NOW?

As a Child of God (which was mentioned in Session 3), you have every opportunity to get to know God because God wants a relationship with you. He wants you to hear His voice and for you to talk with Him. He wants you to tell Him EVERYTHING. He cares about EVERYTHING. So, what do you do now?

Well, as in any relationship, there must be communication. A primary way God communicates is through His Word, the Scriptures. In the Scriptures, He describes Himself, His Kingdom, how He reacts to certain situations, His opinion about things, and His likes and dislikes. When you read the Word, you get to know Him.

There are four gospels in the Bible; four books devoted to telling the story about Jesus and what He did and said while on earth. Why don't you turn to Mathew, Mark, Luke, or John. Pick a passage. Read it and write down what you learn. Also, write down any questions you have after reading the passage. (As you read, if you need more clarity, *Matthew Henry Commentary* is available online for free—www.blueletterbible.org/commentaries/mhc.) For example:

Verse: *John 16:7*
Context: *What Jesus told His disciples before His death.*
The Scripture: *"It is to your advantage that I am going away. For if I do not go away, the [Holy Spirit] will not come to you, but if I go, I will send Him to you."*
Possible Journal Entry: *"God, everything was pre-meditated—Jesus' death, burial, resurrection, and the Holy Spirit coming and dwelling with-*

in the earth. You are a Planner! You've always had a plan. That makes me feel secure and hopeful. I always want to walk in the plans You have for me. Help me to do that."

Now it's your turn. Open the Word and write down what you discover about God. Begin to set aside daily time (five minutes) to develop intimacy with the triune God because as you seek Him, you will find Him in the Word.

Verse:_____

Context:_____

_____

The Scripture:_____

_____

_____

_____

Journal Entry: _____

_____

_____

Conversation Starters with God:

"Lord, I want to commune with You. I want us to be on the same page. Lead me in Your Word. Tell me what makes You happy and what makes You sad. Tell me what is on Your mind. I want to know who You are and how You view the world. What is Your eternal perspective?"

Meditate on These Scriptures & Listen to "No Turning Back":

Then Jesus came up and said to them, "All authority in heaven and on earth has been given to Me. Therefore go and make disciples of all nations, baptizing them in the name of the Father and the Son and the Holy Spirit, teaching them to obey everything I have commanded you. And remember, I am with you always, to the end of the age" (Matt. 28:18-20).

The grace of the Lord Jesus Christ and the love of God and the fellowship of the Holy Spirit be with you all (2 Cor. 13:13).

After Jesus was baptized, just as He was coming up out of the water, the heavens opened and He saw the Spirit of God descending like a dove and coming on Him. And a voice from heaven said, "This is my one dear Son; in Him I take great delight" (Matt. 3:16-17).

But the Advocate, the Holy Spirit, whom the Father will send in My name, will teach you everything, and will cause you to remember everything I said to you (John 14:26).

Session 5:

WHAT'S YOUR ATTITUDE?

After these first four sessions, describe your attitude towards God.

_____

_____

_____

_____

_____

Attitude is everything. Is there still a battle raging in you or are you at peace with the Lord? Are you willing to go the distance with God? Are you willing to do everything He says and leads? This is a huge question.

Since you started this 21-session journey, have you felt the Holy Spirit (the Lord God) trying to communicate to you? What has He been saying? What was your response?

_____

_____

_____

_____

_____

Well, to tell you the truth, if you did not respond positively to the Lord, a change of attitude is needed. If you feel resistance to the Holy Spirit's leading, ask Him what is holding you back and ask for strength to respond in obedience to the Holy Spirit.

Conversation Starters with God:

"God, show me any area in my life where I am resisting You. Also, show me why I am resisting You. I want a vibrant relationship with You."

Meditate on These Scriptures
& Listen to "Anything for You":

You love justice and hate evil. For this reason God, your God has anointed you with the oil of joy, elevating you above your companions (Ps. 45:7).

There is one body and one Spirit, just as you too were called to the one hope of your calling, one Lord, one faith, one baptism, one God and Father of all, who is over all and through all and in all (Eph. 4:4-6).

Finally, brothers and sisters, whatever is true, whatever is worthy of respect, whatever is just, whatever is pure, whatever is lovely, whatever is commendable, if something is excellent or praiseworthy, think about these things. And what you learned and received and heard and saw in me, do these things. And the God of peace will be with you (Phil. 4:8-9).

Trust in the Lord with all your heart, and do not rely on your own understanding (Prov. 3:5).

Humble yourselves before the Lord and He will exalt you (James 4:10).

Part 2:

TIME FOR BREAKTHROUGH

EXPOSE LIES, RECEIVE TRUTH

Deception is the only way that Satan gains power. Authority was given to Adam and Eve, but Satan deceived Eve into thinking that God was trying to prevent a blessing instead of protect them. She knew she was not to eat of the Tree of the Knowledge of Good and Evil, but was deceived into believing that the motivation for that restriction was the desire to prevent her from becoming like a divine being (Gen. 3:1-7). The severe cost of believing and acting on that lie threw Adam and Eve out of the garden, out of God's presence (Gen. 3:8-24).

Most sin originates in a thought, and after meditating on that thought, the thought turns into an action. The demonic voice always deceives, and if you believe that lie, that is where you get into trouble. You may think the voice is saying the truth, but it is really not.

Well, how can you determine whether what you are believing is a lie or not? Look at the fruit.

The Kingdom of God is righteousness, joy, and peace (Rom. 14:7). If what you believe does not cultivate these positive states of being, then it most likely is a lie. For example, if you look at yourself and think "I am so ugly." The question that exposes the lie is: What is the fruit of that thought? If the fruit is depression, feeling down, refraining from social activities, becoming discouraged, or doing things out of anxiousness, the Kingdom of God is not being manifest.

The next step in analyzing that thought is figuring out its source. For this example, it could be: "Well, I do not look like 'that person.'" Who said that "that person" is the standard? What happened? Well, the lie originated in coveting, and the Ten Commandments states that we shall not covet (Ex. 20:1-17). As you can see, the deception gets you into sin. If you did not believe the lie and enter into sin, you would see "that person" and appreciate him/her for whom he/she is, and love yourself for who you are. Do you see from that example how the lie then gets you into sin? In fact, the truth is that you are fearfully and wonderfully made (Ps. 139:14), and the fruit of this truth is joy, self-satisfaction, and gratitude for your Creator.

Deception can occur in all sorts of relationships and situations that result in the removal of the Kingdom of God from the situation. We do not want this! Let us pray that the Lord would expose all lies in our life.

"I do not see righteousness, joy, and peace in the situation involving

_____ . Lord, expose

all the lies I am believing and reveal the truth. I believe the truth is_____

_____, and knowing this brings

(righteousness, joy, peace) into the situation. I am _____

_____because the truth shows me that _____

_____."

"I do not see righteousness, joy, and peace in the situation involving

_____ . Lord, expose

all the lies I am believing and reveal the truth. I believe the truth is_____

_____, and knowing this brings

(righteousness, joy, peace) into the situation. I am _____

_____because the truth shows me that _____

_____."

"I do not see righteousness, joy, and peace in the situation involving

_____ . Lord, expose

all the lies I am believing and reveal the truth. I believe the truth is_____

_____, and knowing this brings

(righteousness, joy, peace) into the situation. I am _____

_____because the truth shows me that _____

_____."

Most times, the lies come in because we do not know our identity. The Scriptures are a great resource that describe who we are in God.

Conversation Starters with God:
"God, what lies am I believing? What is the Truth?"

Meditate on These Scriptures
& Listen to "Child of God":

But to all who have received Him—those who believe in His name— He has given the right to become God's children (John 1:12).

We know that our old man was crucified with Him so that the body of sin would no longer dominate us, so that we would no longer be enslaved to sin (Rom. 6:6).

God created humankind in His own image, in the image of God He created them, male and female He created them (Gen. 1:27).

But you are a chosen race, a royal priesthood, a holy nation, a people of his own, so that you may proclaim the virtues of the One who called you out of darkness into His marvelous light (1 Pet. 2:9).

Or do you not know that your body is the temple of the Holy Spirit who is in you, whom you have from God, and you are not your

own? For you were bought at a price. Therefore glorify God with your body (1 Cor. 6:19-20).

I no longer call you slaves, because the slave does not understand what his master is doing. But I have called you friends, because I have revealed to you everything I heard from My Father (John 15:15).

For we are His workmanship, having been created in Christ Jesus for good works that God prepared beforehand so we may do them (Eph. 2:10).

Who will separate us from the love of Christ? Will trouble, or distress, or persecution, or famine, or nakedness, or danger, or sword? As it is written, "For your sake we encounter death all day long; we were considered as sheep to be slaughtered." No, in all these things we have complete victory through Him who loved us! For I am convinced that neither death, nor life, nor angels, nor heavenly rulers, nor things that are present, nor things to come, nor powers, nor height, nor depth, nor anything else in creation will be able to separate us from the love of God in Christ Jesus our Lord (Rom. 8:35-39).

Session 7:

REPENT

John the Baptist and Jesus repeatedly said, "Repent for the Kingdom of God is at hand" (Matt. 3:2). What does "repent" mean? It is the changing of one's mind: turning 180 degrees away from something and walking fully away from it. We usually repent from a sin, for example, fornication. A non-married person having sexual intercourse with a non-married person would be engaging in fornication. Repentance for that person would entail:

1) recognizing that fornication is a sin,

2) repenting (having Godly sorrow) for engaging in pre-marital sex, and

3) never engaging in that sin again.

In short, fleeing (running away) from that sin—like Joseph fleeing from Potiphar's wife (Gen. 39:12). We can also repent from critical attitudes leading to critical and wounding words. In fact, there are a slew of things we can repent from.

Take a look at Gal. 5:19-21: "Now the works of the flesh are obvious: sexual immorality, impurity, depravity, idolatry, sorcery, hostilities, strife, jealousy, outbursts of anger, selfish rivalries, dissensions, factions, envying, murder, drunkenness, carousing, and similar things. I am warning you, as I had warned you before: Those who practice such things will not inherit the Kingdom of God!"

Look over every work of the flesh listed in Gal. 5:19-21. Is there anything you are struggling with? Do you have Godly sorrow and desire to truly repent? Why don't you repent now and walk out that repentance in the next couple of weeks?

"Lord, I repent for _____."

43

I fully understand and acknowledge that it is a sin and that it breaks Your heart when I engage in it. I am changing my mind concerning _____

_____

_____

_____.

I fully recognize that it is unholy, damaging, and has caused pain. I truly desire to be more like you. Fill me with the knowledge of You and search my heart, Oh Lord. Strengthen me as I walk out my repentance so that there is evidence."

"Lord, I repent for _____.
I fully understand and acknowledge that it is a sin and that it breaks Your heart when I engage in it. I am changing my mind concerning _____

_____

_____

_____.

I fully recognize that it is unholy, damaging, and has caused pain. I truly desire to be more like you. Fill me with the knowledge of You and search my heart, Oh Lord. Strengthen me as I walk out my repentance so that there is evidence."

"Lord, I repent for _____.
I fully understand and acknowledge that it is a sin and that it breaks Your heart when I engage in it. I am changing my mind concerning _____

_____

_____

_____.

I fully recognize that it is unholy, damaging, and has caused pain. I truly desire to be more like you. Fill me with the knowledge of You and search my heart, Oh Lord. Strengthen me as I walk out my repentance so that there is evidence."

"Lord, I repent for _____.
I fully understand and acknowledge that it is a sin and that it breaks Your heart when I engage in it. I am changing my mind concerning _____

_____

_____

_____

_____

_____.

I fully recognize that it is unholy, damaging, and has caused pain. I truly desire to be more like you. Fill me with the knowledge of You and search my heart, Oh Lord. Strengthen me as I walk out my repentance so that there is evidence."

"Lord, I repent for _____.
I fully understand and acknowledge that it is a sin and that it breaks Your heart when I engage in it. I am changing my mind concerning _____

_____

_____

_____.

I fully recognize that it is unholy, damaging, and has caused pain. I truly desire to be more like you. Fill me with the knowledge of You and search my heart, Oh Lord. Strengthen me as I walk out my repentance so that there is evidence."

When repenting, it is wise to look at your current situation and make conscious changes. Do you need to remove items from your home or office? Do you need to remove yourself from social situations? What and whom do you need to surround yourself with? These changes allow the fruit of your repentance to materialize. Jot down the things that you need to change and how you will change them:

_____

_____

_____

_____

_____

_____

_____

_____

_____

Conversation Starters with God:

"Lord, what else do I need to repent from? Show me. Also, Lord, what do I need to change in order for my repentance to materialize in my life? Share with me."

Meditate on These Scriptures & Listen to "Whisper Your Secrets":

Thus it stands written that the Christ would suffer and would rise from the dead on the third day, and repentance for the forgiveness of sins would be proclaimed in His name to all nations, beginning from Jerusalem. You are witnesses of these things (Luke 24:46-48).

Therefore produce fruit that proves your repentance (Matt. 3:8).

Therefore repent and turn back so that your sins may be wiped out, so that times of refreshing may come from the presence of the Lord, and so that He may send the Messiah appointed for you—that is, Jesus (Acts 3:19-20).

Watch yourselves! If your brother sins, rebuke him. If he repents, forgive him (Luke 17:3).

Or do you have contempt for the wealth of his kindness, forbearance, and patience, and yet do not know that God's kindness leads you to repentance? (Rom. 2:4).

Now I rejoice, not because you were made sad, but because you were made sad to the point of repentance. For you were made sad

as God intended, so that you were not harmed in any way by us. For sadness as intended by God produces a repentance that leads to salvation, leaving no regret, but worldly sadness brings about death (2 Cor. 7:9-10).

FORGIVE

Unforgiveness clouds the soul like poor eyesight distorts a driver's view. It garbles vision and makes the journey to the destination harder. In contrast, forgiveness removes hindrances and smoothes out life's journey. Jesus highlights its importance by speaking about it immediately after He shares the "Lord's Prayer." He states, "But if you do not forgive others, your Father will not forgive you your sins" (Matt. 6:15).

In response, your first instinct could be: "I don't have a forgiveness problem." But, let us ask God. Let us pray for self-awareness. Consider these scenarios:

1)   Is there ever a time when you enter a room (conference, reunion, lunch) and you literally "don't see" someone, you are blind to them?

2)   When you think of a situation, does your blood pressure increase, and do you start having contentious conversations with yourself?

3)   If a name is mentioned, do you have to fight to not disparage that person, or is your involuntary reflex to insult the person?

All those situations are showing evidence of unforgiveness.

In certain circumstances, you may think. "I cannot forgive." Ponder Jesus. One of the last words He spoke from the cross included, "Father, forgive them for they don't know what they are doing." Do you think He "felt like forgiving"? After all the injustice, mockery, cruelty He endured. The pain, the blood, His flesh hanging off His body, mangled, unrecognizable, enduring treachery, lies, betrayal. But, He made up His mind (His soul) in the Garden of Gethsemane. His soul was not clouded with unforgiveness.

He had made the choice to forgive.

Let us be sons of God and forgive. The whole earth is waiting for us to manifest (Rom. 8:19). Let us manifest forgiveness—to be truly Christ-like and forgive. Also, let us take it a step further and plead on the behalf of the one who did the injustice — to not only declare forgiveness over them, but to bless them (Matt. 5:44-45).

"Lord, I realize that I've harbored unforgiveness in this situation:

_____

_____

_____.

I want to forgive. Today I release the situation and/or person(s) to you. I forgive _____for _____.
In fact, I pray that you bless him/her/them. Pour out your Spirit upon him/her/them and may they not only know you as Savior and Lord, but also as Friend, Protector, Love, and Counselor."

"Lord, I realize that I've harbored unforgiveness in this situation:

_____

_____

_____.

I want to forgive. Today I release the situation and/or person(s) to you. I forgive _____for _____.
In fact, I pray that you bless him/her/them. Pour out your Spirit upon him/her/them and may they not only know you as Savior and Lord, but also as Friend, Protector, Love, and Counselor."

"Lord, I realize that I've harbored unforgiveness in this situation:

_____

_____

_____.

I want to forgive. Today I release the situation and/or person(s) to you. I forgive _____for _____.

In fact, I pray that you bless him/her/them. Pour out your Spirit upon him/her/them and may they not only know you as Savior and Lord, but also as Friend, Protector, Love, and Counselor."

"Lord, I realize that I've harbored unforgiveness in this situation:

_____

_____

_____ .

I want to forgive. Today I release the situation and/or person(s) to you. I forgive _____for _____.
In fact, I pray that you bless him/her/them. Pour out your Spirit upon him/her/them and may they not only know you as Savior and Lord, but also as Friend, Protector, Love, and Counselor."

"Lord, I realize that I've harbored unforgiveness in this situation:

_____

_____

_____ .

I want to forgive. Today I release the situation and/or person(s) to you. I forgive _____for _____.
In fact, I pray that you bless him/her/them. Pour out your Spirit upon him/her/them and may they not only know you as Savior and Lord, but also as Friend, Protector, Love, and Counselor."

At times, exercising forgiveness opens up old wounds. You may relive painful moments. Be encouraged. Healing follows the pain. Sometimes a doctor has to re-break a bone in order for it to heal correctly. Sometimes we have to re-open a wound and exercise forgiveness in order for our soul wound to completely heal.

Conversation Starters with God:
"God, reveal any and all unforgiveness that may reside in my heart."

Meditate on These Scriptures
& Listen to "No Turning Back":

But if we confess our sins, He is faithful and righteous, forgiving us our sins and cleansing us from all unrighteousness (1 John 1:9).

"Come, let's consider your options," says the Lord. "Though your sins have stained you like the color red, you can become white like snow; though they are as easy to see as the color scarlet, you can become white like wool" (Isa. 1:18).

In Him we have redemption through His blood, the forgiveness of our trespasses, according to the riches of His grace (Eph. 1:7).

For this is My blood, the blood of the covenant, that is poured out for many for the forgiveness of sins (Matt. 26:28).

May my words and my thoughts be acceptable in your sight, O Lord, my sheltering rock and my redeemer (Ps. 19:14).

BREAK AGREEMENT

Have you ever felt like bad things continue to happen or that you cannot break through into a period of blessing? Well, at times this is an indicator that there is some type of agreement with the enemy. Other words for agreement are oath, vow, promise, pact, bond, etc. Awareness of these agreements vary; hence, the importance of asking God to highlight any ungodly agreements in our lives. The enemy of our souls only comes to seek, kill, and destroy (John 10:10), and we must be ever vigilant of his deceptive tactics to get us to enter into agreement with him.

For example, after experiencing an injustice, in anger we can say to ourselves, "I will always hate _____ for the rest of my life." The type of anger and hatred released in an unjust situation is very important. There is righteous anger and righteous hatred (Prov. 8, Ps. 11, Eph. 4:26-27). But unrighteous anger and unrighteous hate actually produce a murderous spirit in our heart (1 John 3:15), and are the manifestation of an agreement with the enemy.

Unrighteous hate and anger breeds bitterness, and nothing good comes from it. The injustice was real; but instead of dealing with it in a righteous manner through agreement with the Lord's truth, we align ourselves with the enemy's hatred and anger. This can be devastating to us the rest of our life. As a result, we must break agreement with the enemy and act accordingly, thus, demonstrating that the agreement has been broken.

For example, instead of being offended at someone's harsh comment, we can reply with a compliment and gift. Another example: Instead of letting internal rage due to an injustice eat up our peace, we can break agreement with the rage, acknowledge the wrong, and make wise decisions that align with God's will. "Love your enemies; seek good for those who revile and curse you" (Luke 6:28).

Consider James' direction: "Therefore submit to God. Resist the devil and he will flee from you" (James 4:7).

When we submit to God, a realignment of covenant occurs. Our covenant with God is like a friendly contract that happens to be eternal: When Party A (us) accepts Party B's (God's) offer of Jesus as Savior and Lord, the two parties create a contract where each party has certain responsibilities and benefits.

God will never break His covenant with us. In God's Covenant, we are covered by the blood of the Lamb, are righteous by His blood, and are in a covenant of peace whereby God dwells inside of us and desires relationship with us. By aligning ourselves with this covenant we are aligning ourselves with what God says about us, our future, and about every situation.

However, we can inject strain, dysfunction, and curses into our side of the covenant by making agreements with the demonic (Deut. 28). The demonic does not bring peace, righteousness, or joy, which are traits of the Kingdom of God (Rom 14:17). As a result, when we see the demonic kingdom manifesting, we must break these agreements in prayer, and cease and desist from any participation or association with them.

So, do you remember making any oaths, promises, vows, pacts, bonds, agreements whether consciously or unconsciously that were not holy and righteous and did not bring joy or peace? Or, do you now realize that unconsciously you have made a demonic agreement? Let's confess it to the Lord and break agreement!

"Lord, I confess that I _____

_____

_____

and I repent. I break all agreement with _____
and I stand on our covenant. This is the only covenant I have except with my (future) spouse. Everything else is broken. In the name of Jesus."

"Lord, I confess that I _____

_____

_____

and I repent. I break all agreement with _____

and I stand on our covenant. This is the only covenant I have except with my (future) spouse. Everything else is broken. In the name of Jesus."

"Lord, I confess that I _____

_____

_____

and I repent. I break all agreement with _____

and I stand on our covenant. This is the only covenant I have except with my (future) spouse. Everything else is broken. In the name of Jesus."

"Lord, I confess that I _____

_____

_____

and I repent. I break all agreement with _____

and I stand on our covenant. This is the only covenant I have except with my (future) spouse. Everything else is broken. In the name of Jesus."

Conversation Starters with God:

"Lord, show me every demonic agreement. I only want to be in agreement and in covenant with You, Lamb of God who took away the sins of the world."

Meditate on These Scriptures
& Listen to "Anything":

Again, I tell you the truth, if two of you on earth agree about whatever you ask, My Father in heaven will do it for you (Matt. 18:19).

The king stood by the pillar and renewed the covenant before the

Lord, agreeing to follow the Lord and to obey His commandments, laws, and rules with all his heart and being, by carrying out the terms of this covenant recorded on this scroll. All the people agreed to keep the covenant (2 Kings 23:3).

No, I mean that what the pagans sacrifice is to demons and not to God. I do not want you to be partners with demons. You cannot drink the cup of the Lord and the cup of demons. You cannot take part in the table of the Lord and the table of demons. Or are we trying to provoke the Lord to jealousy? Are we really stronger than He is? (1 Cor. 10:20-22).

Do not become partners with those who do not believe, for what partnership is there between righteousness and lawlessness, or what fellowship does light have with darkness? And what agreement does Christ have with Beliar? Or what does a believer share in common with an unbeliever? And what mutual agreement does the temple of God have with idols? For we are the temple of the living God, just as God said, "I will live in them and will walk among them, and I will be their God, and they will be my people." Therefore "come out from their midst, and be separate," says the Lord, "and touch no unclean thing, and I will welcome you, and I will be a father to you, and you will be My sons and daughters," says the All-Powerful Lord (2 Cor. 6:14-18).

Therefore do not let sin reign in your mortal body so that you obey its desires, and do not present your members to sin as instruments to be used for unrighteousness, but present yourselves to God as those who are alive from the dead and your members to God as instruments to be used for righteousness (Rom. 6:12-13).

Do not give the devil an opportunity (Eph. 4:27).

But keep away from youthful passions, and pursue righteousness, faithfulness, love, and peace, in company with others who call on the Lord from a pure heart. But reject foolish and ignorant controversies, because you know they breed infighting. And the Lord's slave must not engage in heated disputes but be kind toward all, an apt teacher, patient, correcting opponents with gentleness. Perhaps God will grant them repentance and then knowledge of the truth and they will come to their senses and escape the devil's trap where they are held captive to do his will (2 Tim. 2:22-26).

Be careful not to allow anyone to captivate you through an empty, deceitful philosophy that is according to human traditions and the elemental spirits of the world, and not according to Christ (Col. 2:8).

And in the same way He took the cup after they had eaten, saying, "This cup that is poured out for you is the new covenant in My blood" (Luke 22:20).

Session 10:

ACT IN AN OPPOSITE SPIRIT

"For our struggle is not against flesh and blood, but against the rulers, against the powers, against the world rulers of this darkness, against the spiritual forces of evil in the heavens" (Eph. 6:12).

The truth that we do not wrestle against people should shock your heart to life like a difibulator. An alive heart energetically loves everyone with the understanding that people may be influenced by demonic, unclean spirits. People are not our enemy; the spirits influencing them are. As a Christian, the Holy Spirit grants us a gift of discernment to know the spirit that is in operation in each situation (1 Cor. 12:10). If we have doubts, all we have to do is ask the Holy Spirit: What is influencing this person? Once we have the answer, we can act in an opposite spirit.

Do you realize that one of the best techniques to disarm the influence of a demonic spirit is to respond in the opposite of that spirit? For example, if someone comes up to you and speaks in a rude and offensive manner, responding in a consistent, polite way will diffuse the argumentative spirit. Or, for example, if you hear through the grapevine that someone is saying bad things about you, speaking positive and sincere words concerning that person will diminish the influence of that slandering spirit.

The reason why you can respond in an opposite Spirit is because you have THE SPIRIT OF GOD in you. "What is born of the Spirit is Spirit" (John 3:6). The key: Allow the Spirit within you to birth Spirit-filled responses.

Think about a couple of situations in your life and write down how you can respond in an opposite spirit:

When _____
happens, I resolve with God's grace to flow with the Holy Spirit and act
like _____.

When _____
happens, I resolve with God's grace to flow with the Holy Spirit and act
like _____.

When _____
happens, I resolve with God's grace to flow with the Holy Spirit and act
like _____.

When _____
happens, I resolve with God's grace to flow with the Holy Spirit and act
like _____.

When _____
happens, I resolve with God's grace to flow with the Holy Spirit and act
like _____.

Conversation Starters with God:

"Lord, make me self-aware in every situation so that my responses
will bring your Kingdom, which is peace, righteousness, and joy, in
every situation."

Meditate on These Scriptures
& Listen to "Freedom":

*Now may the God of hope fill you with all joy and peace as you
believe in Him, so that you may abound in hope by the power of
the Holy Spirit (Rom. 15:13).*

*For God does not give us a spirit of fear, but of power and love and
self-control (2 Tim. 1:7).*

For the outlook of the flesh is death, but the outlook of the spirit is life and peace (Rom. 8:6).

Make every effort to keep the unity of the Spirit in the bond of peace (Eph. 4:3).

For you did not receive the spirit of slavery leading again to fear, but you received the Spirit of adoption, by whom we cry, "Abba, Father" (Rom. 8:15).

But I say, live by the Spirit and you will not carry out the desires of the flesh. For the flesh has desires that are opposed to the Spirit, and the Spirit has desires that are opposed to the flesh, for these are in opposition to each other, so that you cannot do what you want. But if you are led by the Spirit, you are not under the law. Now the works of the flesh are obvious: sexual immorality, impurity, depravity, idolatry, sorcery, hostilities, strife, jealousy, outbursts of anger, selfish rivalries, dissensions, factions, envying, murder, drunkenness, carousing, and similar things. I am warning you, as I had warned you before: Those who practice such things will not inherit the kingdom of God! But the fruit of the Spirit is love, joy, peace, patience, kindness, goodness, faithfulness, gentleness, and self-control. Against such things there is no law. Now those who belong to Christ have crucified the flesh with its passions and desires. If we live by the Spirit, let us also behave in accordance with the Spirit (Gal. 5:16-25).

Session 11:

NO DISCUSSION, JUST REBUKE

Have you ever caught yourself having conversations in your head? Ever replayed a conversation or a situation and emotionally started boiling? Have you ever had a favorable disposition towards someone one second, and then, after thinking a specific thought, you felt anger towards them?

Well, consider this: There are three voices: your voice, God's, and the demonic. Since the Kingdom of God's manifestation is peace, joy, and righteousness, if the fruit of your head-discussion is not those three things, then, guess what? You are not talking with God, and if God is not the other person in the conversation, probably best to stop talking. In fact, not only stop talking, but rebuke those thoughts.

When was the last time that, while you were alone and thinking, you became angry, sad, felt neglected, or experienced another negative emotion? Write down the context:

_____

_____

_____

_____

_____

_____

_____

Ok. Judge it. Have you forgiven? If you have forgiven, it is under the blood, so declare it vocally: _____is under the blood. All those negative thoughts must go, in Jesus' name. If you have not forgiven, now is a good time!

Have you given the situation to the Lord? Have you told Him that you need His intervention and His wisdom (James 1:5)? The situation could be completely unjust and you could be completely innocent, but you do not need to remain a mental victim. You can know the truth about the situation, but the Truth of God will set you free to be able to live a kingdom lifestyle of peace, joy, and righteousness.

For any given situation, you may have to take these thoughts captive every few minutes, but gradually, the thoughts will disappear. By casting down these arguments, you will have breakthroughs in every area of your life. Emotionally, you will be steady; physically, you will be healthier (for example, anger increases blood pressure); and mentally, you will be free to meditate on what is right, pure, lovely, admirable, excellent, and praiseworthy (Phil. 4:8).

In fact, why don't you write down some Philippians 4:8 thoughts:

_____

_____

_____

_____

_____

_____

_____

_____

_____

_____

_____

_____

_____

_____

_____

_____

_____

Conversation Starters with God:
"Lord, reveal everything in my soul that does not bear as fruit peace, joy, and righteousness."

Meditate on These Scriptures
& Listen to "Whisper Your Secrets":

For though we live as human beings, we do not wage war according to human standards, for the weapons of our warfare are not human weapons, but are made powerful by God for tearing down strongholds. We tear down arguments and every arrogant obstacle that is raised up against the knowledge of God, and we take every thought captive to make it obey Christ (2 Cor. 10:3-5).

Finally, brothers and sisters, whatever is true, whatever is worthy of respect, whatever is just, whatever is pure, whatever is lovely, whatever is commendable, if something is excellent or praiseworthy, think about these things" (Phil. 4:8).

Guard your heart with all vigilance, for from it are the sources of life (Prov. 4:23).

For no good tree bears bad fruit, nor again does a bad tree bear good fruit, for each tree is known by its own fruit. For figs are not gathered from thorns, nor are grapes picked from brambles. The good person out of the good treasury of his heart produces good, and the evil person out of his evil treasury produces evil, for his mouth speaks from what fills his heart (Luke 6:43-45).

He said, "What comes out of a person defiles him. For from within,

out of the human heart, come evil ideas, sexual immorality, theft, murder, adultery, greed, evil, deceit, debauchery, envy, slander, pride, and folly. All these evils come from within and defile a person" (Mark 7:20-23).

Do not be conformed to this present world, but be transformed by the renewing of your mind, so that you may test and approve what is the will of God—what is good and well-pleasing and perfect (Rom. 12:2).

For those who live according to the flesh have their outlook shaped by the things of the flesh, but those who live according to the Spirit have their outlook shaped by the things of the Spirit. For the outlook of the flesh is death, but the outlook of the Spirit is life and peace, because the outlook of the flesh is hostile to God, for it does not submit to the law of God, nor is it able to do so. Those who are in the flesh cannot please God (Rom. 8:5-8).

Keep thinking about things above, not things on the earth (Col. 3:2).

BE UNOFFENDABLE

"Then He said to the disciples, 'Stumbling blocks [offenses] are sure to come, but woe to the one through whom they come!'" (Luke 17:1).

Offense is inevitable! Even Jesus shares that "[Stumbling blocks [offenses] are sure to come." If you know something is coming your way, then, prepare for it. Offense is certain to come.

What is the big deal about offense? Well, *skandalon*, the transliteration of the Greek word for offense, means, "any person or thing by which one is (entrapped) drawn into error or sin." The problem with offense is that it draws someone into error or sin, and sin separates us from God. We desire to be saturated with the presence of God, not to be devoid of His presence. We desire to be free from sin, not entrapped. We desire to respond to an offense in an opposite spirit, with God's Spirit. So, how do we become "unoffendable, "not easily drawn into error or sin"?

Knowing your value in Christ is vital. You are so valuable to God that He died to have relationship with you. Priceless. He pursued you with such intensity that He suffered for you. He wants you. He enjoys you. Knowing the extent of God's love for you is essential. Nothing can separate you from the Love of God. He wants the best for you. His mercies are new every morning.

Knowing who God is, is also crucial. This God who died (sacrificed Himself) for you, this God who loves you, created the world. He is the Healer, the Provider, the Deliverer, the Savior, the Comforter, the Messiah, Abba Father, Most High, All-Powerful One, the Holy One, and I could go on.

If you know who values and loves you and who you are in Him, you will take the high road, you will walk in the Spirit, and move forward with the Lord, leaving the offense on the side of the road, never having been picked up.

Are there any offenses that need to be left at the side of the road?

"Lord, I realize _____offended me. I do not want to keep this offense. I forgive _____ and I release all bitterness and resentment. Show me if there is anything else to release: _____ I desire to live an unoffendable life. Thank You, Lord, for Your love and support through this."

"Lord, I realize _____offended me. I do not want to keep this offense. I forgive _____ and I release all bitterness and resentment. Show me if there is anything else to release: _____ I desire to live an unoffendable life. Thank You, Lord, for Your love and support through this."

"Lord, I realize _____offended me. I do not want to keep this offense. I forgive _____ and I release all bitterness and resentment. Show me if there is anything else to release: _____ I desire to live an unoffendable life. Thank You, Lord, for Your love and support through this."

"Lord, I realize _____offended me. I do not want to keep this offense. I forgive _____ and I release all bitterness and resentment. Show me if there is anything else to release: _____ I desire to live an unoffendable life. Thank You, Lord, for Your love and support through this."

Conversation Starters with God:
"Lord, reveal when I have been offended, and show me if I still harbor offense. Mold me into a place of such security in You that offenses slide down me like water on a duck's back."

Meditate on These Scriptures & Listen to "Child of God":

I will give you a new heart, and I will put a new spirit within you. I will remove the heart of stone from your body and give you a heart of flesh (Ezek. 36:26).

A fool rejects his father's discipline, but whoever heeds reproof shows good sense (Prov. 15:5).

Therefore, be imitators of God as dearly loved children and live in love, just as Christ also loved us and gave Himself for us, a sacrificial and fragrant offering to God (Eph. 5:1-2).

But I say to you who are listening: Love your enemies, do good to those who hate you, bless those who curse you, pray for those who mistreat you (Luke 6:27-28).

But I say to you, love your enemy and pray for those who persecute you, so that you may be like your Father in heaven, since He causes the sun to rise on the evil and the good, and sends rain on the righteous and the unrighteous (Matt. 5:44-45).

You must put away all bitterness, anger, wrath, quarreling, and slanderous talk—indeed all malice. Instead, be kind to one another, compassionate, forgiving one another, just as God in Christ also forgave you (Eph. 4:31-32).

Session 13:

PRAY THE WORD

The truth is that Christ's death and resurrection has provided us total victory no matter what the situation. The question is: How do we access this victory? The answer is: Pray the Word.

For example, when I struggled with fear, I would pray Isaiah 41:10.

<u>The Scripture:</u>"Your word, Lord, says, 'Don't be afraid, for I am with you! Don't be frightened, for I am your God! I strengthen you—Yes, I help you—Yes, I uphold you with My saving right hand!'"

<u>The Prayer:</u> "Lord, you command me not to fear. I will do as you say and I will not fear. Yes, You are with me. I have the All-Powerful All-Mighty God at my side helping and guiding me. You are with me. If You are with me, there is nothing that can stop me. My focus is on You and only You, Lord...."

Before I could finish praying, all fear would leave. Prayer is powerful!

Just as easily as you can pray for yourself, you can also pray for others. Why don't you practice?

_____is dealing with _____.

The scripture I'm standing on is _____and this

is my prayer as I pray the Word of God over the situation: _____

_____

_____

_____

_____

_____

_____

Specifically, I declare _____

_____(summarize the outcome

you have just prayed for).

_____is dealing with_____.

The scripture I'm standing on is _____and this

is my prayer as I pray the Word of God over the situation: _____

_____

_____

_____

_____

_____

_____

_____

_____

Specifically, I declare_____

_____(summarize the outcome

you just prayed for).

_____is dealing with_____.

The scripture I'm standing on is _____and this

is my prayer as I pray the Word of God over the situation: _____

_____

_____

_____

_____

_____

_____

_____

Specifically, I declare_____

_____(summarize the outcome

you just prayed for).

Consider what the Lord has done for you and what you can bestow not only on yourself but on others. Consider the overcoming power you have through the living Word of God. Pray the Word.

> ## *Conversation Starters with God:*
> "Lord, open your Word to me. One of my desires is to see myself free in certain areas and to see family, friends, and even strangers free. Spirit, invigorate me in praying the Word."

Meditate on These Scriptures & Listen to "No Turning Back":

For the word of God is living and active and sharper than any double-edged sword, piercing even to the point of dividing soul from spirit, and joints from marrow; it is able to judge the desires and thoughts of the heart (Heb. 4:12).

And this is the confidence that we have before Him: that whenever we ask anything according to His will, He hears us (1 John 5:14).

If my people, who belong to Me, humble themselves, pray, seek to please Me, and repudiate their sinful practices, then I will respond from heaven, forgive their sin, and heal their land (2 Chron. 7:14).

When you call out to Me and come to Me in prayer, I will hear your prayers (Jer. 29:12).

Is anyone among you suffering? He should pray. Is anyone in good spirits? He should sing praises (James 5:13).

But I say to you, love your enemy and pray for those who persecute you, so that you may be like your Father in heaven, since He causes the sun to rise on the evil and the good, and sends rain on the righteous and the unrighteous (Matt. 5:44-45).

The Lord abhors the sacrifices of the wicked, but the prayer of the upright pleases Him (Prov. 15:8).

Rejoice in hope, endure in suffering, persist in prayer (Rom. 12:12).

Then Jesus told them a parable to show them they should always pray and not lose heart (Luke 18:1).

Always rejoice, constantly pray, in everything give thanks. For this is God's will for you in Christ Jesus (1 Thess. 5:16-18).

Part 3:

WALKING IN THE SPIRIT

Session 14:

THE POWER OF LOVE

Love is a powerful spiritual weapon. It dismantles the hardest of hearts and shifts atmospheres. God is the source of this power and the Scriptures share how to wield it:

Love is patient, love is kind, it is not envious. Love does not brag, it is not puffed up. It is not rude, it is not self-serving, it is not easily angered or resentful. It is not glad about injustice, but rejoices in the truth. It bears all things, believes all things, hopes all things, endures all things. Love never ends (1 Cor. 13:4-8).

Through this Scripture, the Lord unveils the mystery surrounding love. Write your thoughts concerning each description and discuss how it applies to your life. This may take a while. Take breaks as needed because this journey of love will be rewarding.

Love is patient:

Love is kind:

_____
_____
_____
_____
_____
_____
_____
_____
_____

Love is not envious:

_____
_____
_____
_____
_____
_____
_____
_____
_____

Love does not brag:

_____
_____
_____
_____
_____
_____
_____
_____

THE POWER OF LOVE

Love is not puffed up:

_____

_____

_____

_____

_____

_____

_____

_____

Love is not rude:

_____

_____

_____

_____

_____

_____

_____

_____

Love is not self-serving:

_____

_____

_____

_____

_____

_____

_____

_____

_____

Love is not easily angered or resentful:

_____

_____

_____

_____

_____

_____

_____

Love thinks no evil:

_____

_____

_____

_____

_____

Love is not glad about injustice, but rejoices in the truth:

_____

_____

_____

_____

_____

_____

_____

THE POWER OF LOVE

Love bears all things:

_____

_____

_____

_____

_____

_____

Love believes all things:

_____

_____

_____

_____

_____

_____

_____

Love hopes all things:

_____

_____

_____

_____

_____

_____

Love endures all things:

_____

_____

_____

_____

_____

_____

_____

_____

Love never ends:

_____

_____

_____

_____

_____

_____

As you can see from the Scriptures, Biblical love is an action, not a feeling. Thus, you can love even if you do not "feel" loving by making the choice to love, to do what is listed in 1 Corinthians 13:4-8. Interestingly, God elevates love over faith and hope (1 Cor. 13:13).

Love finds itself front and center in the First and Second Greatest Commandments. The First Commandment: "Love the Lord your God with all your heart, with all your soul, and with all your mind" (Matt. 22:37). The Second Commandment: "Love your neighbor as yourself" (Matt. 22:39). So, love is important to God and His Kingdom. Set yourself on a course of victory: LOVE as mentioned in the First Commandment, Second Commandment, and 1 Corinthians 13:4-8. Let that be your calling card, your defining characteristic.

As a result, consider this question: What hinders you from choosing love? _____

"Lord, I realize that in this situation _____

_____ I continue to not choose love. I realize I do this

because _____,

but your word says love _____

so by Your grace, Lord, I resolve to choose love from now on."

    "Lord, I realize that in this situation _____

_____I continue to not choose love. I realize I do this

because _____,

but your word says love _____

so by Your grace, Lord, I resolve to choose love from now on."

    "Lord, I realize that in this situation _____

_____I continue to not choose love. I realize I do this

because _____,

but your word says love _____

so by Your grace, Lord, I resolve to choose love from now on."

    "Lord, I realize that in this situation _____

_____I continue to not choose love. I realize I do this

because _____,

but your word says love_____

so by Your grace, Lord, I resolve to choose love from now on."

    "Lord, I realize that in this situation _____

_____I continue to not choose love. I realize I do this

because _____,

but your word says love _____

so by Your grace, Lord, I resolve to choose love from now on."

Conversation Starters with God:

"Lord, show me how to love You according to the First Commandment. Show me how to love myself so I can love my neighbor according to the Second Commandment. Lord, show me how to live a 1 Corinthians 13:4-8 life."

Meditate on These Scriptures
& Listen to "Freedom":

Love must be without hypocrisy. Abhor what is evil, cling to what is good (Rom. 12:9).

Now one of the experts in the law came and heard them debating. When he saw that Jesus answered them well, he asked Him, "Which commandment is the most important of all?" Jesus answered, "The most important is: 'Listen, Israel, the Lord our God, the Lord is one. Love the Lord your God with all your heart, with all your soul, with all your mind, and with all your strength.' The second is: 'Love your neighbor as yourself.' There is no other commandment greater than these" (Mark 12:28-31).

Above all keep your love for one another fervent, because love covers a multitude of sins (1 Pet. 4:8).

Dear friends, let us love one another, because love is from God, and everyone who loves has been fathered by God and knows God (1 John 4:7).

There is no fear in love, but perfect love drives out fear, because fear has to do with punishment. The one who fears punishment has not been perfected in love. We love because He loved us first (1 John 4:18-19).

For this is the way God loved the world: He gave His one and only Son, so that everyone who believes in Him will not perish but have eternal life (John 3:16).

THE POWER OF WORSHIP

God surrounds Himself with worship. In His throne room as worship, the 24 elders are casting down their golden crowns and the four living creatures are singing, "Holy, Holy, Holy, is the Lord God, the All-Powerful, who was and who is and who is to come!" (Rev. 4:1-8). His choice to be enveloped in worship is not pride or narcissism: it is the expression of all creation at the revelation of who He is.

Worship of God is directly proportional to your understanding of who He is, your closeness to Him, your intimate knowledge of Him. Worship is not just musical, but it is the position of our heart towards God.

We have the ability to worship the Lord with every breathe as we wash dishes, drive our car, walk to the mail box, etc. The closer you are to Him, the easier you fall into worship. The more you know the truth of God and the closer you are to His Spirit, the deeper you can worship Him.

When approaching Him in worship, we must worship Him by the Spirit He gave us because that is how we know Him. His Spirit revealed Himself to us and we received Him into us. The only thing holy within us is His Spirit within us. Thus, we worship Him by His Spirit. And His Spirit leads us into all truth about Himself.

When we worship Him, we have His full attention. Consider the Greek word for "worship" in the above scripture John 4:24. The Greek word is proskyneō. One of its definitions is to "kiss the hand to (towards) one, in a token of reverence." Kissing someone means that you are in close proximity and that you have their full attention.

When we "kiss the hand of God in reverence," we are in close spiritual contact with Him and we have His full attention. Our King's eyes are always on the one that kisses His hand.

What do you want your worship life to look like?

_____

_____

_____

_____

_____

_____

_____

_____

Conversation Starters with God:

"Oh, Lord, show me how you want to be worshiped. How do you want me to kiss your hand?"

Meditate on These Scriptures
& Listen to "Anything for You":

God is spirit, and the people who worship Him must worship in spirit and truth (John 4:24).

Praise the Lord, O my soul! With all that is within me, praise His holy name! (Ps. 103:1).

I praise You constantly and speak of Your splendor all day long (Ps. 71:8).

For it is written, "As I live, says the Lord, every knee will bow to Me, and every tongue will give praise to God" (Rom. 14:11).

O Lord, You are great, mighty, majestic, magnificent, glorious, and sovereign over all the sky and earth! You have dominion and exalt Yourself as the ruler of all (1 Chron. 29:11).

From the same mouth come blessing and cursing. These things should not be so, my brothers and sisters (James 3:10).

Or do you not know that your body is the temple of the Holy Spirit who is in you, whom you have from God, and you are not your own? For you were bought at a price. Therefore glorify God with your body (1 Cor. 6:19-20).

The Lord is great and certainly worthy of praise! No one can fathom His greatness! (Ps. 145:3).

The crowds that went ahead of Him and those following kept shouting, "Hosanna to the Son of David! Blessed is the one who comes in the name of the Lord! Hosanna in the highest!" (Matt. 21:9).

Because experiencing Your loyal love is better than life itself, my lips will praise You. For this reason I will praise You while I live; in Your name I will lift up my hands (Ps. 63:3-4).

Session 16:

THE POWER
OF SPEAKING LIFE

Sometimes the hardest thing to do is to keep your mouth shut. It would be easier to wrestle a bear than to hold back choice words, but hold back we must.

James 1:26 cuts to the bone on this issue: "If someone thinks he is religious yet does not bridle his tongue, and so deceives his heart, his religion is futile." Who wants their relationship with the Lord to be useless (or any relationship, for that matter)? This scripture is like a sword to the heart. How egregious: to be called out because we are not controlling our tongue.

Note: It does not matter the situation even if it is an unjust situation. We are still called to control our tongue. The power of life and death are in the tongue (Prov. 18:21). God spoke this world into existence. Speaking has creative power. Every word spoken is like a seed sown into souls and the fruit either bears life or death. Whatever is sown will be reaped.

Additionally, whatever is spoken actually reveals your heart. It is like a mirror. If you speak poison, your words reflect your poisonous heart (Matt. 12:34, 15:18; Luke 6:45). If you speak sweet words of affirmation or lovingly tough words of truth, your words reflect your healthy heart.

What have you been speaking over other people's lives or situations? Have you been encouraging, uplifting, and positive? Or have you been negative, cursing, tearing down, gossiping, and releasing anger and bitterness? Have you asked to see the situation through God's eyes?

Why don't you dialogue with the Lord concerning this issue:

"Lord, I desire to speak life in every situation. I notice that I am not speaking life when _____

_____

_____

_____

_____

_____

_____

I do not want to do this any more. In fact, I am going to write down the life I should be speaking in this situation. Lord, please give me the words, the scripture, and Your perspective concerning this."

_____

_____

_____

_____

_____

_____

"Lord, I desire to speak life in every situation. I notice that I am not speaking life when _____

_____

_____

_____

_____

_____

I do not want to do this any more. In fact, I am going to write down the life I should be speaking in this situation. Lord, please give me the words, the scripture, and Your perspective concerning this."

_____
_____
_____
_____
_____
_____
_____

"Lord, I desire to speak life in every situation. I notice that I am not speaking life when _____

_____
_____
_____
_____
_____

I do not want to do this any more. In fact, I am going to write down the life I should be speaking in this situation. Lord, please give me the words, the scripture, and Your perspective concerning this."

_____
_____
_____
_____
_____
_____

Conversation Starters with God:

"Lord, create in me a pure heart and from this pure heart may I speak life."

Meditate on These Scriptures
& Listen to "Whisper Your Secrets":

But since we have the same spirit of faith as that shown in what has been written, "I believed; therefore I spoke," we also believe, therefore we also speak (2 Cor. 4:13).

Jesus said to them, "Have faith in God. I tell you the truth, if someone says to this mountain, 'Be lifted up and thrown into the sea,' and does not doubt in his heart but believes that what he says will happen, it will be done for him. For this reason I tell you, whatever you pray and ask for, believe that you have received it, and it will be yours" (Mark 11:22-24).

The good person out of the good treasury of his heart produces good, and the evil person out of his evil treasury produces evil, for his mouth speaks from what fills his heart (Luke 6:45).

You must let no unwholesome word come out of your mouth, but only what is beneficial for the building up of the one in need, that it may give grace to those who hear (Eph. 4:29).

Death and life are in the power of the tongue, and those who love its use will eat its fruit (Prov. 18:21).

The one who guards his words guards his life, but whoever is talkative will come to ruin (Prov. 13:3).

Even a fool who remains silent is considered wise, and the one who

holds his tongue is deemed discerning (Prov. 17:28).

I tell you that on the day of judgment, people will give an account for every worthless word they speak (Matt. 12:36).

Do not return evil for evil or insult for insult, but instead bless others because you were called to inherit a blessing (1 Pet. 3:9).

Understand this, my dear brothers and sisters! Let every person be quick to listen, slow to speak, slow to anger (James 1:19).

When words abound, transgression is inevitable, but the one who restrains his words is wise (Prov. 10:19).

I will praise the Lord at all times; my mouth will continually praise Him (Ps. 34:1).

Session 17:

THE BLESSING
OF SACRIFICE

Most people when asked to do something wonder, "What's in it for me?" or they determine "I'm not interested—that's going to take too much time and effort." When you walk in the Spirit, at times the Lord will lead you to do things that to the flesh are uncomfortable, expensive, and time consuming.

Consider the woman who poured a year's worth of wages onto Jesus's feet—the feet were the ugliest part of a person's body, laden with dust, mud, possibly bugs, long toe nails, etc. In fact, even today in the Middle East, to step upon something with one's feet or to turn one's feet towards a person is the highest of insults. This woman not only poured this expensive oil upon His feet, but also washed His feet with her tears and dried them with her hair. This was a sacrifice of dignity, finances, and personal cleanliness, all for the Love of God. She had sinned greatly, was forgiven greatly, and now could love greatly. And love greatly she did! (Luke 7:36-50)

David, similarly, demonstrated a sacrifice of praise as he danced before the ark, dressed only in a loin cloth. He unabashedly danced before all of Israel, basically naked before his God because of his great love for the Lord. He sacrificed dignity, peace with people (even his wife became jealous of him and ridiculed him), privacy, etc., because of His love for God (2 Sam. 6:12-23).

Remember the woman with her two mites? She went, in a very low-key manner, to the temple to give her offering, a substantial financial sacrifice in order to bless God. She did this because she loved God (Luke 21:1-4).

Do you find yourself resisting sacrifice? Resisting doing something from which you may not experience reward while on this earth? Not making decisions based on an eternal perspective?

When you die, the only person you are required to answer to is God. Our parents, spouse, cousins, friends, aunts, and uncles will not be there. It is just you and God. At that moment you will have to face everything you have done, good and bad.

As a Christian, the blood of the Lamb will cover your sins; but then, there is nothing that covers your lack of good works. You will stand before Him utterly exposed in every way, the rewards will be distributed accordingly (Col. 3:23-24; Rom. 2:6; James 1:12; Deut. 5:33; 1 Cor. 3:11-15; Rev. 2:7, 17, 26-28; Rev. 3:5, 12, 21; Rev. 22:12; etc.).

Take some time and talk with God about the times when you have felt His nudging. How have you responded? Would you respond differently now?

_____

_____

_____

_____

_____

_____

_____

_____

Conversation Starters with God:

"Lord, I'm concerned about sacrificing. I acknowledge the battle in my flesh. Help my faith. Help me to know when to sacrifice."

Meditate on These Scriptures
& Listen to "Freedom":

For even the Son of Man did not come to be served, but to serve, and to give his life as a ransom for many (Mark 10:45).

No one has greater love than this—that one lays down his life for his friends (John 15:13).

And live in love, just as Christ also loved us and gave Himself for us, a sacrificial and fragrant offering to God (Eph. 5:2).

To do righteousness and justice is more acceptable to the Lord than sacrifice (Prov. 21:3).

"Go and learn what this saying means: 'I want mercy and not sacrifice.' For I did not come to call the righteous, but sinners" (Matt. 9:13).

Honor the Lord from your wealth and from the first fruits of all your crops (Prov. 3:9).

For even the Son of Man did not come to be served but to serve, and to give his life as a ransom for many (Mark 10:45).

But even if I am being poured out like a drink offering on the sacrifice and service of your faith, I am glad and rejoice together with all of you (Phil. 2:17).

Through him then let us continually offer up a sacrifice of praise

to God, *that is, the fruit of our lips, acknowledging his name* (*Heb. 13:15*).

Therefore I exhort you, brothers and sisters, by the mercies of God, to present your bodies as a sacrifice—alive, holy, and pleasing to God—which is your reasonable service (Rom. 12:1).

THE BLESSING
OF OBEDIENCE

Rebel against sin. Do not rebel against God! Your attitude towards sin should reflect: "Ha! I'm going to be holy! Darkness, you have no place in me. Bam!" Be a rebel with a cause—to live a sinless life, to be one that pushes against darkness because the light of God shines so brightly.

So, how do you turn the brights on inside yourself? It's simple: obey God. When you invite someone into your home, you usually do extra cleaning to make the home look presentable and more confortable. Consider God. He certainly would rather reside within you when you are obedient because obedience keeps you clean from the filth of sin.

Obedience also shows God your love for Him. Being with God is a love relationship. He loves you; you love Him. He died for you; you obey Him; He wants the best for you; you receive His best. Thus, you are blessed! Obeying Him means that you are on the straight path to victory in every area and primed and ready to receive His favor and blessing for your life.

Why don't you write down a love note to God?

_____

_____

_____

_____

_____

_____

Now, take some time and talk to God about the obedience in your life. Are you following the two great commandments? "The most important is: 'Listen, Israel, the Lord our God, the Lord is one. Love the Lord your God with all your heart, with all your soul, with all your mind, and with all your strength.' The second is: 'Love your neighbor as yourself.' There is no other commandment greater than these" (Mark 12:29-31).

So, how are you doing in following these commandments? Have a discussion with the Lord. Are there any hindrances to your obedience? Are you ready to let them go? Is there anything you would like to declare to the Lord? Write it down. Make it plain.

_____

_____

_____

_____

_____

_____

_____

_____

_____

_____

"Lord, I've felt you prompting me to do _____

_____

_____, but instead I've done _____.

I'm sorry. I believe that I've not done it because of _____

_____and that's a lie. The truth is _____

_____."

"Lord, I've felt you prompting me to do _____

_____

_____, but instead I've done _____.

I'm sorry. I believe that I've not done it because of _____

_____ and that's a lie. The truth is _____

_____."

"Lord, I've felt you prompting me to do _____

_____

_____, but instead I've done _____.

I'm sorry. I believe that I've not done it because of_____

_____ and that's a lie. The truth is _____

_____."

"Lord, I've felt you prompting me to do _____

_____

_____, but instead I've done _____.

I'm sorry. I believe that I've not done it because of _____

_____and that's a lie. The truth is _____

_____."

Conversation Starters with God:

"Lord, strengthen me. Help me to do what you are asking me to do. Even if it is hard on my flesh, let me walk in the Spirit and let Your Spirit guide my life."

Meditate on These Scriptures
& Listen to "Anything for You":

Certainly, obedience is better than sacrifice; paying attention is better than the fat of rams (1 Sam. 15:22b).

If you love Me, you will obey My commandments (John 14:15).

But He replied, "Blessed rather are those who hear the word of God and obey it" (Luke 11:28).

Jesus replied, "If anyone loves Me, he will obey My word, and My

Father will love him, and We will come to him and take up residence with him (John 14:23).

If you indeed obey the Lord your God and are careful to observe all His commandments I am giving you today, the Lord your God will elevate you above all the nations of the earth (Deut. 28:1).

But be sure you live out the message and do not merely listen to it and so deceive yourselves (James 1:22).

For just as through the disobedience of the one man many were made sinners, so also through the obedience of one man many will be made righteous (Rom. 5:19).

And we are witnesses of these events, and so is the Holy Spirit whom God has given to those who obey Him" (Acts 5:32).

For all who are led by the Spirit of God are the sons of God (Rom. 8:14).

How blessed is every one of the Lord's loyal followers, each one who keeps His commands! (Ps. 128:1).

THE BLESSING
OF FAITH

"Now without faith it is impossible to please Him: for the one who approaches God must believe that He exists, and that He rewards those who seek Him" (Heb. 11:6).

For 18 Sessions you have been diligently seeking the Lord. Allowing Him to minister to you and focusing your attention upon Him. You did this in faith! You did not see God, but had assurance of whom you wrote, thought, read about, and prayed to. In your heart and soul, you had hope to draw closer to Him: to whisper your secrets to Him and to hear His secrets. Your confidence propelled you forward. You are a living example of faith, and God is pleased.

God's pleasure is amazing. It is not based on results, i.e., performance; it is based on your faith. Faith comes from hearing the Word of God (Rom. 10:17). Did you know there are audio apps, CDs, and DVDs where you can hear the Word of God? Have you ever considered listening to the Word acted out by professional actors as a form of entertainment and yet build your faith simultaneously? This would be a good thing! Would you resolve to obtain one of these options and begin at least listening to the Word? Or would you begin to read out loud the Word as you read it? It could change your life forever.

Here are two excellent websites that facilitate interaction with the Word: biblegateway.com and www.blueletterbible.com. Here are two apps that offer audio of the Bible: Bible.is and The Word of Promise.

Pray about starting a routine of listening to the Word of God. Write out what you would like to do:

_____

_____

_____

_____

_____

_____

_____

_____

_____

_____

Conversation Starters with God:

"Lord, make your Word alive to me. Let it be imprinted upon my soul."

Meditate on These Scriptures
& Listen to "No Turning Back":

I pray that according to the wealth of His glory He may grant you to be strengthened with power through His Spirit in the inner person, that Christ may dwell in your hearts through faith...(Eph. 3:16-17).

For this reason I tell you, whatever you pray and ask for, believe that you have received it, and it will be yours (Mark 11:24).

Now faith is being sure of what we hope for, being convinced of what we do not see (Heb. 11:1).

Now may the God of hope fill you with all joy and peace as you

believe in Him, so that you may abound in hope by the power of the Holy Spirit (Rom. 15:13).

But he must ask in faith without doubting, for the one who doubts is like a wave of the sea, blown and tossed around by the wind (James 1:6).

Now without faith it is impossible to please Him, for the one who approaches God must believe that He exists and that He rewards those who seek Him (Heb. 11:6).

You have not seen Him, but you love Him. You do not see Him now but you believe in Him, and so you rejoice with an indescribable and glorious joy, because you are attaining the goal of your faith— the salvation of your souls (1 Pet. 1:8-9).

But you, as a person dedicated to God, keep away from all that. Instead pursue righteousness, godliness, faithfulness, love, endurance, and gentleness (1 Tim. 6:11).

Jesus said to them, "I am the bread of life. The one who comes to Me will never go hungry, and the one who believes in Me will never be thirsty (John 6:35).

Part 4:

RELY ON THIS

Session 20:

REST ASSURED OF GOD

God says this about Himself:

"The LORD, the LORD, the compassionate and gracious God, slow to anger and abounding in loyal love and faithfulness, keeping loyal love for thousands, forgiving iniquity and transgression and sin. But He by no means leaves the guilty unpunished, responding to the transgression of fathers by dealing with children and children's children, to the third and the fourth generation" (Ex. 34:6-7).

God chose these words to describe Himself to Moses. He could have highlighted His power and strength, His brilliance and creativity, His wealth and prestige; but instead, He highlighted His sensitivity and justice.

God wanted not only Moses to know about his "soft-side" melded with justice, but also wants You to know this. Love poured out is merciful, gracious, longsuffering, and abounding in goodness and truth, while not ignoring the guilty. God is love poured out, literally and figuratively. As children because of Christ's blood spilled, we can repent and not experience the consequences of the guilty, but experience a merciful, gracious, longsuffering, and abounding in goodness and truth God.

I feel a shout of praise boiling within me. The Lord, my God, is a GOOD, GOOD FATHER. He has saved me, delivered me, healed me, loved me, kept me, protected me, and I could go on and on.

Take some time and write down what you are thankful for. Talk to your merciful and gracious Father. Let Him write a story of redemption and restoration on your heart.

_____

_____

_____

_____

_____

_____

_____

_____

_____

_____

_____

_____

_____

_____

_____

_____

_____

_____

_____

_____

_____

Conversation Starters with God:
"Lord, reveal to me all of You."

Meditate on these Scriptures *& Listen to "Child of God":*

God is not a man, that He should lie, nor a human being, that He should change His mind. Has He said, and will He not do it? Or has He spoken, and will He not make it happen? (Num. 23:19).

For the Lord your God is a consuming fire; He is a jealous God (Deut. 4:24).

For the Lord your God is God of gods and Lord of lords, the great, mighty, and awesome God who is unbiased and takes no bribe, who justly treats the orphan and widow, and who loves resident foreigners, giving them food and clothing (Deut. 10:17-18).

For the Lord your God goes with you to fight on your behalf against your enemies to give you victory (Deut. 20:4).

"I am the God of Abraham, the God of Isaac, and the God of Jacob?" He is not the God of the dead but of the living! (Matt. 22:32).

Every word of God is purified; he is like a shield for those who take refuge in him (Prov. 30:5).

Do not be deceived. God will not be made a fool. For a person will reap what he sows, because the person who sows to his own flesh will reap corruption from the flesh, but the one who sows to the Spirit will reap eternal life from the Spirit (Gal. 6:7-8).

And we have come to know and to believe the love that God has in us. God is love, and the one who resides in love resides in God, and God resides in him (1 John 4:16).

Session 21:

LISTEN TO
THE HOLY SPIRIT

For the rest of your life, the question to ask: What is the Holy Spirit saying? And for the rest of your life, you can expect answers. The Holy Spirit desires for you to engage Him. He wants to talk with you. He is God, and God is into you. When something involves you, nothing is too trivial. He truly wants to be your best friend, and there are serious perks with being best friends with the most powerful being in the universe.

Perk #1: He Knows Everything

As God, the Holy Spirit is omniscient—He knows everything. This is very advantageous for you because "He will guide you into all truth" (John 16:13). In order to be successful in anything, you need to know "the truth." If you want to buy a stock, you need to know "the truth" about the growth potential of the company. If you desire to marry, since He knows the heart and mind of your potential mate, He is an excellent matchmaker. He knows when it will rain and where a traffic accident will be. He can save you time and your hair and clothes from being soaked. He is the Spirit of wisdom, understanding, counsel, might, knowledge, and fear of the Lord (Isa. 11:2). When you are hooked up with The Source, you will lack for nothing. Now, that is awesome.

Perk #2: He is Here to Help

The Holy Spirit is the steady friend you can lean upon as you walk life out (John 16:7). He is here to help you, to co-labor with you, to never leave you or forsake you. He is here to comfort you, to intercede for you, to teach and to remind you what Jesus Christ has said. His desire is for you to be free from all oppression and for you to accomplish His will for your life. He is here to help you go from "glory to glory." He is here to help you to be victorious in every aspect of your life. With a Helper like the Holy Spirit, you can only move forward and never backwards.

Perk #3: He is Not a "Yes" Man

The Holy Spirit is straightforward and will not lie to you. There is no manipulation or deception in His being, so He will not use you. He will tell you what you need to know and when. If you are making a mistake, He will tell you. If you are heading to a place of danger, He will tell you. "He will prove the world wrong concerning sin and righteousness and judgment" (John 16:8-9).

Take some time to pray and journal.

"Holy Spirit, I look forward to hearing You today. Thank You ahead of time for guiding me, helping me, and giving me everything I need in order to do life for today. I would love to know what You are saying right now; so, Holy Spirit, please share Your heart with me."

_____

_____

_____

_____

_____

_____

"Holy Spirit, I realize that you know everything, all truth! I have a couple of questions for You, and I believe You will answer them:"

_____

_____

_____

_____

_____

_____

_____

_____

_____

"Holy Spirit, I need some help in these areas:"

_____

_____

_____

_____

_____

_____

_____

"Holy Spirit bluntly tell me where I need to straighten things in my life, and also feel free to tell me countless times a day how much You love me."

_____

_____

_____

_____

_____

_____

_____

_____

_____

_____

_____

_____

_____

Conversation Starters with God:
"Holy Spirit, I am flat out excited that You dwell inside me and that You are my Counselor and Guide. Talk with me. I am listening."

Meditate on These Scriptures
& Listen to "Whisper Your Secrets":

But I am full of the courage that the Lord's Spirit gives, and have a strong commitment to justice. This enables me to confront Jacob with its rebellion, and Israel with its sin (Mic. 3:8).

And because you are sons, God sent the Spirit of His Son into our hearts, who calls "Abba! Father!" (Gal. 4:6).

Do you not know that you are God's temple and that God's Spirit lives in you? (1 Cor. 3:16).

Or do you not know that your body is the temple of the Holy Spirit who is in you, whom you have from God, and you are not your own? (1 Cor. 6:19).

Moreover if the Spirit of the one who raised Jesus from the dead lives in you, the one who raised Christ from the dead will also make your mortal bodies alive through His Spirit who lives in you (Rom. 8:11).

Protect that good thing entrusted to you, through the Holy Spirit who lives within us (2 Tim. 1:14).

But when He, the Spirit of truth, comes, He will guide you into all truth. For He will not speak on His own authority, but will speak whatever He hears, and will tell you what is to come (John 16:13).

For you did not receive the spirit of slavery leading again to fear, but you received the Spirit of adoption, by whom we cry, "Abba, Father" (Rom. 8:15).

But the fruit of the Spirit is love, joy, peace, patience, kindness, goodness, faithfulness, gentleness, and self-control. Against such things there is no law (Gal. 5:22-23).

Appendix

LYRICS

FREEDOM

© & ℗ 2016 Natasha

VERSE 1:

Despite what I've done, He loves me.

Despite what I've said, He whispers sweet promises.

Despite what I've been through, He never left my side.

Despite who I am, He loves me.

PRE-CHORUS:

So, I declare

CHORUS:

Freedom. Freedom. Freedom to love. Freedom to trust.

VERSE 2:

Despite where I run, He finds me.

Despite who I love, He patiently waits for me.

Despite the pain I cause, He always forgives me.

Despite who I am, He still loves me.

BRIDGE:

Nothing can separate.

Nothing can separate.

Nothing, Nothing can separate me from His love.

Nothing can separate.

Nothing can separate.

Nothing can separate, separate me from His love.

WHISPER YOUR SECRETS

© & ℗ 2016 Natasha

PRE-INTRO:
Ba-ba-ba-ba

INTRO:
Some think He'll come in lightening and thunder.
Some think He'll come with earth shaking rumbles
Some think He'll come with fierce winds.
But He comes as a whisper from within.

Ba-ba-ba-ba

PRE-CHORUS:
The Lord lives in me. Christ lives in me.
His Spirit lives in me. He's whispering.

VERSE 1:
I wanna know Your heart. I wanna know Your thoughts.
I wanna be, I wanna be Your best friend.
Let's go away to the secret place.
I wanna hear Your voice, calling me by name. So...

CHORUS:
Whisper Your secrets, Lord. Tell me about the hidden things.
Reveal Your mysteries to me. Yeah Yeah
Whisper Your secrets, Lord. Tell me about the hidden things.
Reveal Your mysteries to me.

VERSE 2:
I wanna know Your heart. I wanna know Your thoughts.
I wanna be, I wanna be Your best friend.
I wanna know Your plans. I wanna walk in Your ways.
I'm gonna live for You, all my days.

BRIDGE:
Whisper (vamp)

Chorus 2:
Whisper Your secrets. Tell me about the hidden.
Reveal Your mysteries to me.
Whisper Your secrets. Tell me about the hidden.
Reveal Your mysteries to me. Ohhhhh

Verse 3 & 1:
I wanna know Your heart. I wanna know Your thoughts.
I wanna be, I wanna be Your best friend.
Hold my hand.
Let me rest in Your embrace and
Dance through this life, face to face.
I wanna know Your heart. I wanna know Your thoughts.
I wanna be, I wanna be Your best friend.
Let's go away to the secret place.
I wanna hear your voice, calling me by name.

Ba-ba-ba-ba

CHILD OF GOD

CHORUS 1:
I am a Child of God, bought by the blood.
Child of God, saved by the Son.
I am a Child of God, Jesus set me free.
Child of God, He delivered me.
He delivered me.

VERSE:
So, I can walk His way, talk His way, sing His way, praise His way.
Know His way, grow His way, love His way, pray His way,
every single day.

CHORUS 2:
I am a Child of God, clothed in His praise.
Child of God, healed in Jesus' name.
I am a Child of God, I stand in righteousness.
Child of God, heavenly blessed
I'm heavenly blessed.

VERSE:
So, I can walk His way, talk His way, sing His way, praise His way.
Know His way, grow His way, love His way, pray His way,
every single day.

BRIDGE:
I celebrate a covenant.
Celebrate everlasting love.
Celebrate Father and His only begotten Son.
My Lord Jesus. Oh, the power of His blood.
I believe in Him.
I'm a Child, Child of God.
A Child of God.
Child of God.

CHORUS 1 & 2 COMPILED:
I am a Child of God, bought by the blood.
Child of God, saved by the Son.
I am a Child of God. Jesus set me free.
Child of God, He delivered me.
I am a Child of God, clothed in His praise.
Child of God, healed in Jesus' name.
Child of God, I stand in righteousness.
A Child of God, I'm heavenly blessed.
I'm heavenly blessed.

NO TURNING BACK

VERSE 1:
I'm bold, I'm strong in Him I serve.
Dedicated, consecrated to His Word.
Sanctified from my mamma's womb
I've hit the point of no return.

My eyes, my thoughts steadfastly rest
On His promises I'm heavenly blessed.
Our covenant—solid—can't break.
Yes, I'm going all the way.

CHORUS:
There's no turning back.
No turning back.   X2

VERSE 2:
I'm young, I'm ready in the Spirit to soar.
Hungry for intimacy with my Lord.
Within a flame of passion burns.
I've hit the point of no return.

My heart, my soul captured by grace.
I long for His presence face to face.
I know this world will fade away.
Yes, I'm going all the way.

BRIDGE:
The world has no ties to me.
I'm free. So free.
To live the dreams He placed in me.
I'm free. So free.
Get ready world. Here I come.
This is how the West was won.
I'm riding to the rising sun.
My life has just begun.

CHORUS & *vamp on "I'm going all the way."*

ANYTHING FOR YOU

© & ℗ 2016 Natasha

VERSE 1:
Like a desert craving water, I thirst for you. I thirst for You.
Like a fragrance drifting to heaven, I draw near to you. I draw near to
You.

CHORUS:
I'll do anything, You want me to. I'll do anything, for You.
I'll do anything, just tell me, Lord. I'll do anything, for You.

VERSE 2:
Like an olive crushed for its oil. I'm broken for You, Lord. I'm broken for
You.
Like a sunrise brings forth new life. I burn for You. I burn for You.

CHORUS:
And...I'll do anything, You want me to. I'll do anything, for You.
I'll do anything, just tell me, Lord. Anything, anything for You.

BRIDGE:
Waiting here before You
Outstretched arms
Open heart.
Humbly imploring You
Have Your way.
Have Your way.

VERSE 3:
Like a newborn weak flesh, spirit strong.
Strengthen me, Lord. Strengthen me, Lord.
Like a new song touch my lips & I am gone.
Send me, Lord. Send me Lord.

CHORUS:
Anything, You want me to. Anything, for You.
I'll do anything, just tell me, Lord. Anything, anything for You.
I'll do anything, You want me to. Anything, for You.
I'll do anything, just tell me, Lord. Anything, for You.